After All

Books by William Matthews

POETRY
Ruining the New Road
Sleek for the Long Flight
Sticks & Stones
Rising and Falling
Flood
A Happy Childhood
Foreseeable Futures
Blues If You Want
Selected Poems and Translations, 1969–1991
Time & Money
After All

PROSE
Curiosities

After All

LAST POEMS

William Matthews

A MARINER BOOK
HOUGHTON MIFFLIN COMPANY
Boston New York

First Mariner Books edition 2000

For information about permission to reproduce selections from
this book, write to Permissions, Houghton Mifflin Company,
215 Park Avenue South, New York, New York 10003.

Visit our Web site: www.hmco.com/trade.

Library of Congress Cataloging-in-Publication Data
Matthews, William, 1942–1997.
After all : last poems / William Matthews.
p.   cm.
ISBN 0-395-91340-3
ISBN 0-618-05685-8 (pbk.)
I. Title.
PS3563.A855A69   1998
811'.54—dc21   98-22909   CIP

Book design by Lisa Diercks
Printed in the United States of America

DOW 10 9 8 7 6 5 4 3 2 1

Some of the poems in this book have appeared in the following publications:
ACM (Another Chicago Magazine): Frazzle. *The Atlantic Monthly:* Dire Cure; No
Return; The Shooting. *Black Warrior Review:* Big Tongue. *Brilliant Corners:*
Mingus in Shadow. *Crab Orchard Review:* Finn Sheep; Oxymorons; Rescue. *Double
Take:* Morningside Heights, July; A Poetry Reading at West Point; Promiscuous.
Five Points: Inspiration; Manners; Hotel St. Pierre, Paris, 1995. *The Gettysburg
Review:* Euphemisms; Mingus in Shadow. *Hubbub:* People Like Us. *Many
Mountains Moving:* Ice Follies. *The Marlboro Review:* Trees in Harold Baumbach's
Paintings. *The Nation:* Rocas del Caribe, Isla Mujeres, 1967; Hotel Raphael,
Rome, 1987. *New England Review:* Prescience. *The New Yorker:* Bucket's Got a
Hole in It; The Cloister; Truffle Pigs; Vermin. *The Ohio Review:* The Bar at the
Andover Inn; Memory; Dog Days; Willow, Weep for Me. *Poetry:* The Place on
the Corner; A Serene Heart at the Movies; Job Interview; Misgivings. *Quarterly
West:* Sooey Generous. *Shenandoah:* Le Quatre Saisons, Montreal, 1979. *Slate:*
Care. *Solo:* Defenestrations in Prague. *Third Coast:* Thinking About Thinking.

for Celia

Contents

Mingus in Shadow

What you see in his face in the last
photograph, when ALS had whittled
his body to fit a wheelchair, is how much
stark work it took to fend death off, and fail.
The famous rage got eaten cell by cell.

His eyes are drawn to slits against the glare
of the blanched landscape. The day he died,
the story goes, a swash of dead whales
washed up on the Baja beach. Great nature grieved
for him, the story means, but it was great

nature that skewed his cells and siphoned
his force and melted his fat like tallow
and beached him in a wheelchair under
a sombrero. It was human nature,
tiny nature, to take the photograph,

to fuss with the aperture and speed, to let
in the right blare of light just long enough
to etch pale Mingus to the negative.
In the small, memorial world of that
negative, he's all the light there is.

Morningside Heights, July

Haze. Three student violists boarding
a bus. A clatter of jackhammers.
Granular light. A film of sweat for primer
and the heat for a coat of paint.
A man and a woman on a bench:
she tells him he must be psychic,
for how else could he sense, even before she knew,
that she'd need to call it off? A bicyclist
fumes by with a coach's whistle clamped
hard between his teeth, shrilling like a teakettle
on the boil. I never meant, she says.
But I thought, he replies. Two cabs almost
collide; someone yells *fuck* in Farsi.
I'm sorry, she says. The comforts
of loneliness fall in like a bad platoon.
The sky blurs—there's a storm coming
up or down. A lank cat slinks liquidly
around a corner. How familiar
it feels to feel strange, hollower
than a bassoon. A rill of chill air
in the leaves. A car alarm. Hail.

The Place on the Corner

No mirror behind this bar: tiers of garish
fish drift back and forth. They too have routines.
The TV's on but not the sound. Dion
and the Belmonts ("I'm a Wanderer") gush
from the box. None here thinks a pink slip
("You're fired," with boilerplate apologies)
is underwear. None here says "lingerie"
or "as it were." We speak Demotic
because we're disguised as ordinary
folks. A shared culture offers camouflage
behind which we can tend the covert fires
we feed our shames to, those things we most fear
to say, our burled, unspoken, common language—
the only one, and we are many.

Rescue

To absolve me of my loneliness, and rather
than board her for the stint, I brought
my cat with me for two weeks in Vermont. Across
bare, borrowed floors she harried ping-
pong balls, her claws like castanets, her blunt face rapt—
she kept a ball ahead of her
and between her paws as she chased it full tilt.

Then she'd amble over to where I sat reading
and stretch her utmost length against
my flank and let her heartbeat diminish until
she dozed. So long as she knew where
in that strange space I was, and up to what, she could
make it hers. When I stepped into
eclipse behind an opaque shower curtain, not

at all like the translucent booth she peers into
to watch the blur lather and rinse
himself at home, and when I turned a different
torrent loose, she must have leapt
to the lid of the toilet tank, and measured what next,
rocking back on her haunches,
then forward, and back again, and then the flying

hoyden launched herself at the rod the shower curtain's
strung along, landing, *clank*, only two
or three inches off, and hung there held up by her
forearms, if a cat has forearms,
like the least fit student in gym class quitting on
a chin-up. Her rear paws churned egg-
beater style. And then what? If I pulled her toward

me with wet, soapy hands, she'd thrash and slash herself
free, but free in a tub. Hung up
as she was, she had nothing to push off from, so
she'd have to let herself drop, *clunk*,
and turn to the torn curtain her I-meant-to-do-
that face, while, slick and pink, I called
out from the other side, "Sweet cat, are you OK?"

Truffle Pigs

None of these men, who all run truffle pigs,
compares a truffle to itself. "Fossil
testicles," says one. And another: "No.
Inky, tiny brains, smart only about
money." They like to say, "You get yourself

a pig like this, you've got a live pension."
The dowsing sows sweep their flat snouts across
the scat and leaf rot, scurf and duff, the slow
fires of decay. They know what to ignore;
these pigs are innocent of metaphor.

Tumor, fetus, truffle—all God's creatures
jubilate to grow. Even the diffident truffle
gives off a faint sweat from the joyful work
of burgeoning, and by that spoor the pigs
have learned to know them and to root them out.

Rocas del Caribe, Isla Mujeres, 1967

Broke, we went when no one else would, July,
and got a corner room. "The wind," the desk
clerk grinned, spreading his arms full span, "will frisk
your room." I'm sure that's what I heard him say.
Breeze surged through the room like gossip. The fear-
fueled calf we shared the ferry with was on
the menu every night. We ate in town.
"*Camarones?*" "Shrimp." It can take a year
twice for a week's vacation: first you save
that long for it and then it lasts that long.
The stubborn surf broke into spume and lace
above the rocks. Bored silly face to face,
we told each other there was nothing wrong,
but filled with dread like a pair of sieves.

Manners

"Sweetypants," Martha Mitchell (wife of John
Mitchell, soon to be Nixon's attorney general)
cried, "fetch me a glass of bubbin,
won't you?" Out of office, Nixon
had been warehoused in Leonard Garment's
New York law firm and had begun to clamber

his way back toward Washington.
The scent of his enemies' blood rose
hotly from the drinks that night.
Why was I there? A college class-
mate's mother had suggested he invite a few
friends; she called us "starving scholars."

It's hard to do good and not advertise
yourself, and not to need the needy
even if they don't need you. I'd grown used
to being accused of being somewhere else.
I plied my nose, that shrewd scout, into book
after book at home, and clattered downstairs

for dinner not late but tardy. I dwelt
as much as I could at that remove
from the needs of others we call "the self,"
that desert isle, that Alcatraz from which
none has escaped. I made a happy lifer.
There is no frigate like a book.

"Outside of a dog, a book is a man's
best friend," said Groucho Marx. "Inside of a dog,

it's too dark to read." So what if my friend's
mother was a fool. So what if Martha
Mitchell would later rat on her rat
of a husband when Nixon's paranoid

domain collapsed under its own venal
weight and it took Nixon all his gloomy
charisma to load his riven heart
onto a helicopter and yaw upward
from the White House lawn. He might have turned
to Pat and asked, like a child on a first

flight, "Are we getting smaller yet?"
I was too young to know how much I was,
simply by being born, a hostage
to history. My hostess's chill,
insulting grace I fended off with the same
bland good manners I used to stay upstairs

in my head until time had come for food.
A well-fed scholar, I sought out and brought
back a tall bubbin for the nice lady.
Yes, there's a cure for youth, but it's fatal.
And a cure for grace: you say what you mean,
but of course you have to know what that is.

The Shooting

It be the usual at first.
This one be bad, that one be worse.

They do this in slow commotion.
They strut, they fuss, something they done

or never done be what they set
fire to and slow turn into fast

because a gun come out and then
gun two, gun three, guns all around

like walls. That mean we be the room.

Prescience

Bloated and mesmerized by raspberries,
the possum wobbled into the open
as you or I might blink into the sun
from an afternoon movie, and because
remembered time is instantaneous,
I hear the rifle slash the silence now,
and smell the nitrate and shattered bowels
and spangled berries, and hear, next, a hiss—
the exhaust of a possum's life and a tithe,
a levy of breath from each who stood there
with nothing better to say than "Got it."
How old was I that stark day? Seven? Eight?
That hiss? I could hear me growing older,
rueful, guarded and sullen for dear life.

Vermin

"What do you want to be when you grow up?"
What child cries out, "An exterminator!"?
One diligent student in Mrs. Taylor's
class will get an ant farm for Christmas, but
he'll not see industry; he'll see dither.
"The ant sets an example for us all,"
wrote Max Beerbohm, a master of dawdle,
"but it is not a good one." These children
don't hope to outlast the doldrums of school
only to heft great weights and work in squads
and die for their queen. Well, neither did we.
And we knew what we didn't want to be:
the ones we looked down on, the lambs of God,
blander than snow and slow to be cruel.

Memory

We're not born knowing how to love the world,
but squalling. The first two years of our lives
crucially form our psyches, but we have
no memory of them. Well, a few shards

perhaps: a ladybug, the gray underside
of a bright leaf, a pixeled mother
murmuring from inside a screen door.
When all we have are fragments, they suffice.

On the debris of rock, on sand, we build
our church, the Little Chapel of the Dunes.
Soon enough it's harder to forget than
to keep track. How steadily the past fills

with what the present could or would not use.
Our silos teem with corn and avid rats.
How will we love the world? We can't forget
what we never knew; we'd better improvise.

"The farther we go, the more we give up,"
we could complain, but there's always more
to lose. The vacuum that dearth abhors
is dearth. We all drink from a leaking cup.

Promiscuous

"Mixes easily," dictionaries
used to say, a straight shot from the Latin.
Chemists applied the term to matter's
amiability.

But the *Random House Dictionary*
(1980) gives as its prime meaning:
"characterized
by frequent and indiscriminate

changes of one's sexual partners." Sounds
like a long way
to say "slut," that glob of blame we once threw
equally at men and women, all who slurred,

slavered, slobbered,
slumped, slept or lapsed, slunk or relapsed, slackened
(loose lips sink ships) or slubbed, or slovened. But soon
a slut was female. A much-bedded male

got called a ladies' man; he never slept
with sluts. How sluts
got to be sluts is thus a mystery,
except the language knows what we may

have forgot. "Depression" began its career
in English in 1656, says
the *OED*,
and meant (science jargon) the opposite

of elevation—a hole or a rut,
perhaps, or, later, "the angular
distance of a celestial object
below the horizon,"

as *Webster's Third* (1963)
has it. There's ample record of our self-
deceit: language,
that furious river, carries on its foamed

and sinewed back all we thought we'd shucked off.
Of course it's all
pell-mell, head over heels, snickers and grief,
love notes and libel, fire and ice. In short:

promiscuous.

Le Quatre Saisons, Montreal, 1979

East from Vancouver I'd rattled across
Canada by train, sitting up all night
to watch the moon-limed Rockies. The wheat
provinces I slept through. I read *Bleak House*
a third time, slowly, fondly. The early
summer sun, "subdued to what it works in,
like the dyer's hand," glinted greenly from
leaves, needles, lakes and regiments of baby
crops. Then, finally, Montreal. I rushed
my mouth out for relief from rail cuisine.
Then in my tasteful room the regrets came
out like chummy ghosts. This far from home
I'd dragged my glum retinue—venal, mean-
spirited, restless and subdued to dust.

No Return

I like divorce. I love to compose
letters of resignation; now and then
I send one in and leave in a lemon-
hued Huff or a Snit with four on the floor.
Do you like the scent of a hollyhock?
To each his own. I love a burning bridge.

I like to watch the small boat go over
the falls — it swirls in a circle
like a dog coiling for sleep, and its frail bow
pokes blindly out over the falls' lip
a little and a little more and then
too much, and then the boat's nose dives and butt

flips up so that the boat points doomily
down and the screams of the soon-to-be-dead
last longer by echo than the screamers do.
Let's go to the videotape, the news-
caster intones, and the control room goes,
and the boat explodes again and again.

Sooey Generous

Saint Anthony, patron of sausage makers,
guide my pen and unkink my tongue. Of swine
I sing, and of those who tend and slaughter them,
of slops and wallows and fodder, of piglets
doddering on their stilty legs, and sows
splayed to offer burgeoned teats to sucklers,
and the four to five tons of manure
a pig (that ambling buffet) reinvests
in the soil each year; of truffle dowsers
and crunchers of chestnuts and acorns I sing.

In medieval Naples, each household
kept a pig on a twenty-four-foot tether,
rope enough that the hooved Hoover could
scour the domain, whereas in Rome
pigs foraged the streets haunted today by
rat-thin cats, tendons with fur. In Paris
in those years the *langueyers*, the "tonguers,"
or meat inspectors, lifted a pig's tongue
to look for white ulcers, since the comely
pig in spoiled condition could poison

a family. Indeed the Buddha died
from eating spoiled pork, vegetarians
I know like to insist, raising the stakes
from wrong to fatal, gleefully. Perhaps
you've read the bumper sticker too: *A Heart
Attack Is God's Revenge for Eating His
Little Friends.* Two major religions
prohibit eating pork. Both creeds were forged

in deserts, and the site-specific pig,
who detests dry mud, has never mixed well

with nomads or vice versa. Since a pig
eats everything, just as the cuisines that
sanctify the pig discard no fragment
of it, it makes sense to eat it whole hog
or shun it altogether, since to eat
or not to eat is sacral, if there's a choice
in the matter. To fast is not to starve.
The thirteen ravenous, sea-queasy pigs
Hernando de Soto loosed near Tampa
in 1542 ate whatever

they liked. How glad they must have been to hoove
some soil after skidding in the slick hold
week after dark week: a pig without sun
on its sullied back grows skittish and glum.
Pigs and pioneers would build America.
Cincinnati was called Porkopolis
in the 1830s; the hogs arrived,
as the hunger for them had, by river,
from which a short forced march led to slaughter.
A new country travels on its belly,

and manufacture starts in the barnyard:
hide for leather and stomach for pepsin.
In France, a farm family calls its pig
"Monsieur." According to a CIA
tally early in 1978,

the Chinese kept 280 million
of the world's 400 million pigs;
perhaps all of them were called "The Chairman."
Emmaeus, swineherd to Odysseus,
guarded 600 sows and their litters

(the males slept outside), and no doubt each sow
and piglet had its own name in that rich
matriarchal mire. And I like to think
that in that mild hospice future pork roasts
fattened toward oblivion with all
the love and dignity that husbandry
has given up to be an industry,
and that the meat of Emmaeus's coddled
porkers tasted a little sweeter for
the graces of affection and a name.

Poem Ending with a Line from John Berryman

One to a corner, the orderly whores
array themselves at the outskirts of Rome.
July. Cicadas. A few cars dawdle
past and then a few of those stop and come back.
Sales are hard when you're also the product.
"I understand, *cara*," one charmer says

to Luisa, who'd rather eat ground glass
than hear some oaf from Lucca call her *cara*,
"my line of work is similar to yours."
Luisa doesn't ask. She does the job
and then she's out of his Fiat and back
on the corner straightening her stockings,

ridiculous as they are in this heat.
Some of the girls, as they call each other,
are Nigerian. They wear white and shine
like buffed coal against the browning grasses
at the periphery of Rome. To men
who hire whores from their cars, "exotic" means

nobody you'd meet on your job or need
to answer to. A wife is like a walk
and a whore like a taxi, thinks Carlo.
Let's invite his wife and a whore of his
choosing to discuss his homely similes
and publish the transcript in *Woman's Day*.

Is it to ease or ensure loneliness
that Carlo and the Luccan drive their cars

away from the Rome toward which all roads
converge in the hopeful formula?
There's not much traffic either way. *I saw
nobody coming, so I went instead.*

A Serene Heart at the Movies

She strode to her car and turned the key and
a peony of bomb bloomed all at once.
The film is rated R for violence.
Dear fellow readers of the *Iliad*,
they found half her pinkie in the roses.
Guns are the jewelry of men. And cars—
think how much the script must have hated her
to blow her up in the burgundy Rolls.
But she's not real; it's only a movie.
Those blood-drenched dreams we wake from in a baste
of sweat, like our sex fantasies, aren't real
to moral life. They don't impede at all
the love we make, the money, or the haste.
So hush now, little baby, don't you cry.

Inspiration

Rumpled, torpid, bored, too tasteful to rhyme
"lethargy" with "laundry," or too lazy,
I'll not spend my afternoon at the desk
cunningly weaving subjunctives and lithe
skeins of barbed colloquial wire. Today

I loathe poetry. I hate the clotted,
dicty poems of the great modernists,
disdainful of their truant audience,
and I hate also proletarian
poetry, with its dutiful rancors

and sing-along certainties. I hate
poetry readings and the dreaded verb
"to share." Let me share this knife with your throat,
suggested Mack. Today I'm a gnarl, a knot,
a burl. I'm furled in on myself and won't

be opened. I'm the bad mood if you try
to cheer me out of I'll smack you. Impasse
is where I come to escape from. It takes
a deep belief in one's own ignorance;
it takes, I tell you, desperate measures.

Hotel St. Pierre, Paris, 1995

I rose six floors in one of those birdcage
ascenseurs the stairs spiraled around,
then laid exhausted claim to my small room.
Swimming upstream against my French all day
at a translation conference had done
me in: the ghettos of English and sleep
welcomed their son back from Babel, at least—
maybe from Babble. I showered and flung
my rented windows open to lure some
cool air in while I dreamed I couldn't find
someplace I knew so well I ached. I woke
to find a pigeon taloned to my toe,
his crimson-ringed eyes staring into mine,
both of us restive, mute and not at home.

Oxymorons

Summer school, and *jumbo shrimp,* of course.
Friendly fire, famous poet, common sense,
and, until very recently, *safe sex.*
Blind date, sure thing, amicable divorce.

Also there's *loyal opposition,*
social security, deliberate speed.
How about *dysfunctional family?*
Eyes blackened, hearts crushed, the damn thing functions.

Some things we say should coat our tongues with ash.
Drug-Free School Zone? No way: it's our money
our children toke, snort and shoot up while we
vote against higher property taxes.

Want a one-word oxymoron? *Prepay.*
Money's—forgive me—rich in such mischief:
trust officer, debt service, common thief—
these phrases all want to have it both ways

and sag at the middle like decrepit beds.
Religious freedom — doesn't that sound good?
And some *assisted living* when we're old
and in our cryptic dreams the many dead

swirl like a fitful snow. We'll wake and not
think of our *living wills* or property.
We'll want some breakfast. Our memories
will be our *real estate,* all that we've got.

Dire Cure

"First, do no harm," the Hippocratic
Oath begins, but before she might enjoy
such balm, the docs had to harm her tumor.
It was large, rare and so anomalous
in its behavior that at first they mis-
diagnosed it. "Your wife will die of it
within a year." But in ten days or so
I sat beside her bed with hot and sour
soup and heard an intern congratulate
her on her new diagnosis: a children's

cancer (doesn't that possessive break
your heart?) had possessed her. I couldn't stop
personifying it. Devious, dour,
it had a clouded heart, like Iago's.
It loved disguise. It was a garrison
in a captured city, a bad horror film
(*The Blob*), a stowaway, an inside job.
If I could make it be like something else,
I wouldn't have to think of it as what,
in fact, it was: part of my lovely wife.

Next, then, chemotherapy. Her hair fell
out in tufts, her color dulled, she sat laced
to bags of poison she endured somewhat
better than her cancer cells could, though not
by much. And indeed, the cancer cells waned
more slowly than the chemical "cocktails"
(one the bright color of Campari), as the chemo
nurses called them, dripped into her. There were

three hundred days of this: a week inside
the hospital and two weeks out, the fierce

elixirs percolating all the while.
She did five weeks of radiation, too,
Monday to Friday like a stupid job.
She wouldn't eat the food the hospital
wheeled in. "Puréed fish" and "minced fish" were worth,
I thought, a sharp surge of food snobbery,
but she'd grown averse to it all—the nurses'
crepe soles' muffled squeaks along the hall,
the filtered air, the smothered urge to read,
the fear, the perky visitors, flowers

she'd not been sent when she was well, the room-
mate (what do "semi-private" and "extra
virgin" have in common?) who died, the nights
she wept and sweated faster than the tubes
could moisten her with pretty poison.
One chemotherapy veteran, six
years in remission, chanced on her former
chemo nurse at a bus stop and threw up.
My wife's tumor has not come back.
I like to think of it in Tumor Hell,

strapped to a dray, flat as a deflated
football, bleak and nubbled like a poorly
ironed truffle. There's one tense in Tumor Hell,
forever, or what we call the present.
For that long the flaccid tumor marinates
in lurid toxins. Tumor Hell Clinic

is, it turns out, a teaching hospital.
Every century or so, the way
we'd measure it, a chief doc brings a pack
of students round. They run some simple tests:

surge current through the tumor, batter it
with mallets, push a woodplane across its
pebbled hide and watch a scurf of tumor-
pelt kink loose from it, impale it, strafe it
with lye and napalm. There might be nothing
left in there but a still space surrounded
by a carapace. "This one is nearly
dead," the lead doc says. "What's the cure for that?"
The students know: "Kill it slower, of course."
They sprinkle it with rock salt and move on.

Here on the aging earth the tumor's gone:
my wife is hale, though wary, and why not?
Once you've had cancer, you don't get headaches
anymore, you get brain tumors, at least
until the aspirin kicks in. Her hair's back,
her weight, her appetite. "And what about you?"
friends ask me. First the fear felt like sudden
weightlessness: I couldn't steer and couldn't stay.
I couldn't concentrate: surely my spit would
dry before I could slather a stamp.

I made a list of things to do next day
before I went to bed, slept like a cork,
woke to no more memory of last night's
list than smoke has of fire, made a new list,

began to do the things on it, wept, paced,
berated myself, drove to the hospital
and brought my wife food from the take-out joints
that ring a hospital as surely as
brothels surround a gold strike. I drove home
rancid with anger at her luck and mine—

anger that filled me the same way nature
hates a vacuum. "This must be hell for you,"
some said. Hell's not other people: Sartre
was wrong about that, too. *L'enfer, c'est moi?*
I've not got the ego for it. There'd be
no hell if Dante hadn't built a model
of his rage so well, and he contrived to
get exiled from it, for it was Florence.
Why would I live in hell? I love New York.
Some even said the tumor and fierce cure

were harder on the caregiver—yes, they
said "caregiver"—than on the "sick person."
They were wrong who said those things. Of course
I hated it, but some of "it" was me—
the self-pity I allowed myself,
the brave poses I struck. The rest was dire
threat my wife met with moral stubbornness,
terror, rude jokes, nausea, you name it.
No, let her think of its name and never
say it, as if it were the name of God.

Euphemisms

Let's skip those undertakers love, like *pass
away* and *join the majority.*
Likewise let's spurn the tittery genteel,
like *make water* or *ladies of the night.*
Why *make water* and not *tinkle?*
I like the uric whiff of Genesis,

the combination of false modesty
and grandeur. Instead, let's think how class
works, and deference, on the British
woman who spoke mildly to the police
of "the gentleman who raped me." Is that
what language is for, to bring us to our knees?

How about phrases without opposites,
like *legal ethics* or *natural world?*
Also, surely, *the right to bear arms.*
What fun it is to scorn those who'd rather
sound right than think. I count among the charms
of feeling superior to them that

it makes us the same fools we think they are:
one touch of smugness makes the whole world kin.
We need to unlearn what we think we know
lest we spool on like answering machines
until we choke on chatter. Who says so?
Not I. English itself murmured this prayer.

Umbrian Nightfall

The stench-rich stones dogs parse all day will reek
all night of data, but one
by one the dogs get summoned home. Streetlights
sizzle on and bats unfurl.
The Tiber valley, trough of a thousand
shades of green, has brimmed with dusk.
It's late. High time. High ground. Even the hill-
top towns stand tiptoe. The lake
of the black night laps everywhere. Two dogs
(three?), like raddled islands, bark.

Hotel Raphael, Rome, 1987

The roof garden? Closed. Bettino Craxi
paced those leafy ramparts at his leisure
whenever the senate sat. Prime minister
then, he's now charged with erasing the faint line
between bribery and coalition
in Italian politics. Two sweet-
faced carabinieri patrolled the street
below, toting automatic weapons.
Between the garden and the guns we dozed
off half our jet lag, then rose for dinner.
The heat the stones had taken in all day
they next gave slowly back at just the pace
it took to stoke the night air thick and humid,
tending the simmer until the sun rose.

Finn Sheep

I had a month at a writers' retreat,
a castle in Midlothian. Some days
I wrote steadily and well, but others
I stalled and moped, surrounded by damp sheep
and scowling at a blank sheet of paper.
"Ravish me," the paper begged. "Not now," I said,
"I've got a headache."

Days that slack, I learned, I could better spend
in Edinburgh. From the bus's upper
deck I could peer over the hedgerows into
people's yards and fields, where, before the bus
left the country for the suburbs, I saw
some astonishing sheep with canoe-shaped ears
like a jackrabbit's,

so long they seemed glued on for a cruel
prank—unwieldy ears that ought to crumple
from their weight and bad design, but won't.
Mottled black and white, the sheep lifted from
the daze of grazing their mild curious
faces and goofy ears as the bus
sputtered past. "Does that,"

they seemed to need to know, "concern me? No?
Well then . . ." And I needed to know the name
of such a sheep, because I never met
a fact I didn't like. And because it's not
that I believe *in* words, but I believe

by words. Suppose I began a sentence,
"I love . . . ," and didn't

know what to say next, my tongue grown torpid,
cobbled by rust? Well then, who would I be?
I rode the bus back to the country starved
for a name. Next day I asked at the castle
and in the village what those sheep were called.
"They're peculiar sheep," the butcher told me,
"I don't know their name."

The librarian said, "Let's ask a shepherd."
She looked one up in the Yellow Pages
and I told him what I'd seen. "Those," he said,
"are Finn sheep, and they're dumb as dung." Their own,
I assumed, unless all dung—each pellet,
dowel, coil or flop, no matter from what
species (each would give

according to its ability)—was equal.
I thought such things while I thanked him and hung
up. I had the fact I'd frothed with greed for,
I'd felt smarter for a millisecond—
a swift spasm of intelligence,
and then I was dumb again and happy
to moil at my desk.

Job Interview

> Think you, if Laura had been Petrarch's wife,
> He would have written sonnets all his life?
>
> —*Don Juan*, III, 63–4

"Where do you see yourself five years from now?"
the eldest male member (or is "male member"
a redundancy?) of the committee
asked me. Not here, I thought. A good thing I

speak fluent Fog. I craved that job like some
unappeasable, taunting woman.
What did Byron's friend Hobhouse say after
the wedding? "I felt as if I had buried

a friend." Each day I had that job I felt
the slack leash at my throat and thought what was
its other trick. Better to scorn the job than ask
what I had ever seen in it or think

what pious muck I'd ladled over
the committee. If they believed me, they
deserved me. As luck would have it, the job
lasted me almost but not quite five years.

Defenestrations in Prague

1419. Angry Protestants stormed
the town hall and tossed Catholic council
members out the window. Those who survived
the fall were sped to the next life by pikes.
Of course Catholics were busy burning
heretics at one stake or another.
Did he who first learned to keep fire wait long
to think how crisp it might singe his neighbor?

1618. Three Catholics fell some
fifty feet from a palace window
to land on a dung heap and live to slink
away and thank God for landing in shit.
One side's miracle, the other's mistake.
Sides? Sides demean the vast loneliness
of prayer—no answer, no neighbor, and death
flickering in you like a pilot light.

Ice Follies

The pavements got glazed with ice, and the brick
walks in particular were wicked slick.
You can hear your fellow citizens fall
all across Ann Arbor—startled vowels
blossom like tardy parachutes
from their fallen bodies. You know how dis-

aster unites people? I wobble,
you teeter, he she or it topples
and we all fall down. You've got to get right
back on the horse after you're thrown, they say.
But what if you're also the horse? The spry
spring back upright: ho ho what a jolly

winter. But the claudicators, the lace-
boned, the seven-months-pregnant, and the lame
all stare mournfully at the slick glitter.
Hardly the quick, not yet the dead, they fear
the very earth turning beneath their feet.
What? What? The meek shall inherit the what?

Dog Days

Qui me amat, amat et canem meam.

—Saint Bernard de Clairvaux (1090–1153)

The cat spends most of them under the bed.
Because July, named after Julius
Caesar, had thirty-one days, August,
named after Augustus Caesar, had to have
thirty-one days, too, and so a day got
filched from February. Only the top

dog (Canis Major, the Romans called
the constellation) gets the day promised
to Everydog, and in the proverb "day"
is singular. A lacy caul of sweat
ensheathes us as we sleep and the wind stalls
and the reluctant dust won't deign to budge,

and all this nothing-going-on goes on
for weeks. Bugs scrawl their bodies on the air.
Nature's last green is brown, the dun mantilla
the hills wrap themselves in when the nights cool
down or off, which is it? The cat looks up
from torturing a bug and then eats it.

Spent Light

Summer solstice in Alaska: light shone
all night long but the birds knew that dawn came
at 2:33 A.M. for then they
lifted their diverse beaks and urged into
the bright, mosquito-freckled air
their Babel of song, not broad- but narrow-

cast to whom it may concern: the furtive vole,
rumpled moose, florid tourist, obdurate
mountain. Their music laved what it "fell on,"
the way we say the hungry fell on food,
light on landscape or the wolf on the fold.
Stars fell on Alabama. A felon

fell on his ass in the prison yard
and his fellow felons made a joyful
noise, a rougher music than birds produce,
but so is almost all the music we have.
"Let there be light," God famously implored,
and the dark released a few hostages.

The Cloister

The last light of a July evening drained
into the streets below. My love and I had hard
things to say and hear, and we sat over
wine, faltering, picking our words carefully.

The afternoon before I had lain across
my bed and my cat leapt up to lie
alongside me, purring and slowly
growing dozy. By this ritual I could

clear some clutter from my baroque brain.
And into that brief vacancy the image
of a horse cantered, coming straight to me,
and I knew it brought hard talk and hurt

and fear. How did we do? A medium job,
which is well above average. But because
she had opened her heart to me as far
as she did, I saw her fierce privacy,

like a gnarled, luxuriant tree all hung
with disappointments, and I knew
that to love her I must love the tree
and the nothing it cares for me.

A Poetry Reading at West Point

I read to the entire plebe class,
in two batches. Twice the hall filled
with bodies dressed alike, each toting
a copy of my book. What would my
shrink say, if I had one, about
such a dream, if it were a dream?

Question-and-answer time.
"Sir," a cadet yelled from the balcony,
and gave his name and rank, and then,
closing his parentheses, yelled
"Sir" again. "Why do your poems give
me a headache when I try

to understand them?" he asked. "Do
you want that?" I have a gift for
gentle jokes to defuse tension,
but this was not the time to use it.
"I try to write as well as I can
what it feels like to be human,"

I started, picking my way care-
fully, for he and I were, after
all, pained by the same dumb longings.
"I try to say what I don't know
how to say, but of course I can't
get much of it down at all."

By now I was sweating bullets.
"I don't want my poems to be hard,

unless the truth is, if there is
a truth." Silence hung in the hall
like a heavy fabric. Now my
head ached. "Sir," he yelled. "Thank you. Sir."

People Like Us

When the ox was the gray enemy
of the forest and engine of the plow,
the poor drifted across the fields,
through the sweet grasses and the vile,
and tendered bare bowls at our doors.
We hoarded and they begged. We piled
ricks high with hay and they slept there
like barn cats or cuckoos.

When we sluiced the maculate streets
with fermenting slops, and strode to our jobs
furred by coal dust, didn't the poor
punctuate our routines with cries
for alms? Our sclerotic rivers
turned the color of old leather
and the poor fished them anyway
and slept under their bridges.

Now they come surging up the stairs
and up the fire escapes. Open our door
to them and then they're us,
and if we don't we're trapped inside
with only us for company
while in the hall they pray and sing
their lilting anthems of reproach
while we bite our poor tongues.

Frazzle

"All for one and one for all" was our motto after all
our tribulations. And then we'd each go home, after all.

By the people. For the people. Of the people. Grammar—
but politics is an incomplete sentence, after all.

"Better to have loved and lost . . . ," the poet wrote.
Than to have won? Poetry dotes on loss, after all.

They don't take the flag down at dusk, the patriot grumbled.
A country's too big to love, but not a rule, after all.

How would you translate "self-service" or "lube job"
if you had a dirty mind and scant English, after all?

Veil (beekeeper's? bridal?), Vale (tears?), Vail (Colorado).
Phonics? No avail. Better learn to spell, after all.

The love of repetition is the root of all form?
Well, liturgy and nonsense are cousins, after all.

"I cannot tell a lie," he said, which was a lie,
but not the kind for which the bill comes after all.

The Bar at the Andover Inn

May 28, 1995

The bride, groom (my son), and their friends gathered
somewhere else to siphon the wedding's last
drops from their tired elders. Over a glass
of chardonnay I ignored my tattered,
companionable glooms (this took some will:
I've ended three marriages by divorce
as a man shoots his broken-legged horse)
and wished my two sons and their families
something I couldn't have, or keep, myself.
The rueful pluck we take with us to bars
or church, the morbid fellowship of woe—
I've had my fill of it. I wouldn't mope
through my son's happiness or further fear
my own. Well, what instead? Well, something else.

Big Tongue

The spit-sheathed shut-in, sometimes
civil, lolls on its leash in its cave
between meals, blunt little *feinschmecker*.
He seems both sullen and proud, not
an unusual combination. Well, that little
blind boy knows his way around the mouth.
An aspirate here, a glottal stop there—
he's a blur. He works to make sensible
noise at least as hard as an organist,
and so giddily pleased by his own

skill that for the sheer bravura
of it he flicks a shard of chicken
salad free from a molar *en route*
to the startling but exact finish
of a serpentine and pleasing sentence.
God knows the brain deserves most
of the credit for the sentence, but then
wasn't it God who insisted from the first
that whatever "it" means, it isn't fair?
Theology can be stored in a couplet:

The reason God won't answer you
is God has better things to do.

I mention only briefly, *mia diletta*,
lest I embarrass you by lingering,
how avidly this tongue nuzzled your nub,
how slowly (glib is his day job) he urged
your pleased clamor. Think then how he might feel—

the spokesman, the truffle pig, Mr. Muscle—
to sense along the length of his savor
a hard node, like a knot in a tree, and thus
to know another attack's begun. First one
side of the bilateral tongue will stiffen

and swell to two or three times normal size
(it's like having a small shoe in your mouth),
and then, as it subsides, after three or four
hours, the other side grows grandiose.
(Your salivary glands are like grapes
on steroids. Your speech is feral—only vowels,
and those from no language you recognize.)
Pride goeth before a bloat. Start to puff yourself up
and next thing you know you'll be on TV,
in the Macy's parade. *Vae, puto deus fio*

("Damn, I think I'm becoming a god," said
the emperor Vespasian on his deathbed).

But let's bring this descant back down to earth:
names ground us, and this humiliation's called
angioedema, short (?!) for angioneurotic
edema, often "an expression of allergy,"
as *Webster's Third* has it. What's the humbled
tongue, sore from strenuous burgeon and wane,
allergic to? Whatever it is, it may well be
systemic, and the "attack" a kind of defense,
a purge, a violent recapture of balance,
like a migraine or an epileptic seizure.

"Who needs this?" I might cry out. The answer
might be: I do. So why am I exchanging vows
with my allergies? Although I hate it when my
competence is sick, I hereby refuse
to make mine allegorical, though not before,
you'll note, I've had my fun with that possibility—
for where's "the bribe of pleasure" (as Dr. Freud,
that gloomy *mensch*, called it) in being sick
if I can't loll in limelight for a while?
Where next? My dressing room, to wipe off the drama

and stare at the mirror,
met by ordinary fear.

Trees in Harold Baumbach's Paintings

"I'm blue," you might say, and I'd know what you mean,
close enough. "My love is a red, red rose,"
you might say, and I'd know you meant chalice,
blood, thorns, swift seasons of bloom and long ones
of memory, and that you didn't mean
she or he had but one green leg and stood

a stubborn ground till death. These frond-like trees
can almost float in the marine colors
they illuminate. They have no roots: beneath
the paint there's only canvas on which they've
been carefully trapped by paint, like flies by
flypaper. And where would they go, where else

could they live? This is the only place some-
one made them and made them and when he'd made them
right, let the paint dry them to the future.
Of course you might have meant by "my love"
not your sweetie but the flame itself. You
might have said, "My love is a tall, pale fire."

Willow, Weep for Me

Same idea as "Cry Me a River,"
really: because nobody gives a fig
for your parochial pain, you enlist
nature to lament for you. All outdoors
commands attention. Of course the other half
of the planet lies swaddled in sleep
and darkness, but all the outdoors you can

see from where you stand means to most people
all the outdoors worth mention. A window
box bristling with herbs isn't nature. God
made nature and humans ruined it. Thus
nature might lament its own demise
in its time free from hymning human grief.
The rushes would sway and stones dance in place

and the willow trail its mournful tresses.
There was always a twinkle in nature's
eye when it sang of Cindy's perfidy—
who'd lean an ounce of trust on Cindy?—
but to sing not as a subcontractor
but in one's own sad stead would set the whole
broken heart of nature to music.

Bucket's Got a Hole in It

Keep it under your hat, the saying went
when we wore hats. And secrets dissipate
(in this poem the verb means "to leave the pate")
like body heat. And some secrets can't quit
memory fast enough for human good;
viz., what my friend's wife's kisses tasted like

and why I didn't sleep with her for all
her vernal allure. Did we need to read
in transcript each taped word of Nixon's
contempt for us, like preserved globs of spit?
Don't double-click on the Save icon
(a piggy bank? a jumbled attic?)

until you've thought how much a fossil fuel
has to forget fossil to become fuel,
or how much childhood we plow under.
"Tears, idle tears," the poet wrote, but they've
got their work cut out for them, the way
a river might imagine a canyon.

Thinking About Thinking

The purpose of art is to save us from truth,
Nietzsche thought, perhaps because he feared
the purpose of truth was to save us from art.
I don't feel in such constant peril, except
perhaps from the urge I have to know what
I think and then say it over and over
like a cupiditous schoolboy using a new
word in a sentence. Suppose what we think
we know proved instead to be a chance
to think again. For example: the cat
walks by itself, but not to the dinner bowl.
Or: even paranoids have real enemies,
and, likewise, mirrors. Or: the cut worm
forgives the plow, twice. My love says I think
too damn much and maybe she's right.
The sorrow of thought is that it replaces
the world that stunned us into thought,
and leads us not to awe but to new
morose connections between language
and desire. So is the purpose of my love
to save me from thinking? I think not.
And this time, for once, she agrees.

Misgivings

"Perhaps you'll tire of me," muses
my love, although she's like a great city
to me, or a park that finds new
ways to wear each flounce of light
and investiture of weather.
Soil doesn't tire of rain, I think,

but I know what she fears: plans warp,
planes explode, topsoil gets peeled away
by floods. And worse than what we can't
control is what we could; those drab,
scuttled marriages we shed so
gratefully may augur we're on our owns

for good reasons. "Hi, honey," chirps Dread
when I come through the door, "you're home."
Experience is a great teacher
of the value of experience,
its claustrophobic prudence,
its gloomy name-the-disasters-

in-advance charisma. Listen,
my wary one, it's far too late
to unlove each other. Instead let's cook
something elaborate and not
invite anyone to share it but eat it
all up very very slowly.

Care

The lump of coal my parents teased
I'd find in my Christmas stocking
turned out each year to be an orange,
for I was their sunshine.

Now I have one C. gave me,
a dense node of sleeping fire.
I keep it where I read and write.
"You're on chummy terms with dread,"

it reminds me. "You kiss ambivalence
on both cheeks. But if you close your
heart to me ever, I'll wreathe you in flames
and convert you to energy."

I don't know what C. meant me to mind
by her gift, but the sun returns
unbidden. Books get read and written.
My mother comes to visit. My father's

dead. Love needs to be set alight
again and again, and in thanks
for tending it, will do its very
best not to consume us.